COGNITIVE FACTOR

HOW OUR BRAIN DISTORTS REALITY

GUIDE TO 99 COGNITIVE BIASES

SATISH GAIRE

Book Organizer *by* Nikesh Chapagain
Book Interior *by* Pankaj Runthala
Book Cover *by sesareyang*
Inspired *by* Elon Musk's Tweet

First Edition

Dedicated to my parents,   Shiv & Laxmi Gaire.
Thank you for everything ♥

Love Satish

Labor Omnia Vincit

Get Exclusive Content Online
CognitiveFactor.net

CONTENTS

MEANING

TIME

WHAT ARE COGNITIVE BIASES

Cognitive biases are like little shortcuts that our brains take when we're making decisions or judgments. You can think of them like a little trick that your brain plays on you, without you even realizing it.

Sometimes these shortcuts are helpful, because they can help us make decisions quickly and easily. For example, if you touch a hot stove, your brain will quickly tell you to pull your hand away, without you having to consciously think about it.

But other times, these shortcuts can lead us to make mistakes in our thinking.

There are many different types of cognitive biases, but they all have one thing in common: they're little ways that our brains can be tricked into thinking something that might not be true.

In this book, we will explore the major ones that might be hindering how you think.

HOW TO USE THIS BOOK

Understand your own logics: By learning about cognitive biases, you can gain insight into how your own mind works and become more aware of the mental shortcuts and biases that may influence your decision-making.

Making better decisions: By recognizing and avoiding common cognitive biases, you can make more informed and rational decisions, especially in situations where emotions or cognitive shortcuts may lead you astray.

Improving communication: Understanding cognitive biases can also help you communicate more effectively with others by recognizing the biases that may be influencing their thinking or behavior.

Identifying biases in others: Finally, by learning about cognitive biases, you can also become more skilled at recognizing biases in others, which can be useful in situations such as negotiations or when evaluating arguments and claims made by others.

In short, learning about cognitive biases can help you become a more effective thinker and decision-maker, both in your personal and professional life.

 Satish Gaire

INFORMATION

HICK'S LAW

More options leads to harder decisions

DESCRIPTION:

Hick's Law, also known as the Hick-Hyman Law, is a psychological principle that describes the relationship between the number of choices presented to a person and the time it takes for them to make a decision. According to this law, the more options someone has, the longer it takes for them to make a decision.

HERE ARE A FEW EXAMPLES TO ILLUSTRATE THIS CONCEPT:

Restaurant menus: Been to a restaurant with an extensive menu and found it difficult to decide what to order?   That's because the more options you have to choose from, the longer it takes to make a decision.

Apple vs Others: Apple utilizes this tactic by having limited product while it's competitors have hundreds to choose from.

Cognitive Factor

2 CONFIRMATION BIAS

People look for evidence that confirms what they think

DESCRIPTION:

The tendency to interpret new evidence as confirmation of one's existing beliefs or theories. Most people have their own specific beliefs on every aspect of life and it clouds them from seeing the real truth because they only see what they already believe in.

This is why political campaigners focus on making their existing base show up for voting rather than trying to convince the other party because their base already believes what they have to say. As a marketer, you should not force too much to change someones mind, rather sell products/services that fuels their belief

EXAMPLE: A person who believes that global warming is real may be more likely to believe news reports that confirm their beliefs, and less likely to believe reports that contradict their beliefs. This is an example of confirmation bias.

PRIMING

INFORMATION

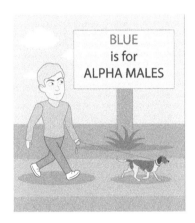

Previous stimuli influence users' decision

DESCRIPTION:

If you expose a person to information over and over, it influences how they make their decisions. Priming can also be put to use by associating a brand with goodwill such as climate change advocates, and status.

This is why Retargeting ads work so well because it exposes a person who has seen your product multiple times which forces them to make a "logical conclusion" to act.

FUN FACT: If you are shown a picture of a smiling face before taking a test, you may be more likely to score higher because you are in a positive mood.

Cognitive Factor

COGNITIVE LOAD

The total amount of mental effort that is required to complete a task

DESCRIPTION:

"Cognitive load" relates to the amount of information that working memory can hold at one time. Since working memory has a limited capacity, instructional methods should avoid over-loading it with additional activities that don't directly contribute to learning. A high cognitive load can lead to errors and decreased performance.

EXAMPLE: A person who is trying to remember a list of items while also trying to pay attention to a conversation may have a high cognitive load and may have difficulty remembering all the items on the list.

PRACTICAL TIP: A lot of people make a 10+ to-do list to have a "productive" day but end up not getting anything done because their brain cannot handle it, instead, try to focus on doing only 2-3 main things a day.

Satish Gaire

ANCHORING BIAS

Users rely heavily on the first piece of information they see

DESCRIPTION:

Anchoring bias is a cognitive bias that occurs when people rely too heavily on the first piece of information they receive when making decisions. The initial information acts as an anchor, influencing their subsequent judgments and decisions.

EXAMPLES:

Pricing: A store offers a product with an original price of $100, but then they put it on sale for $50. Even though the sale price is still high, customers may feel like they're getting a great deal.

Salary Negotiation: If the employer offers a relatively low starting salary, the candidate may then negotiate for only a slightly higher salary, thinking that it's still an improvement over the initial offer.

Cognitive Factor

6

NUDGE

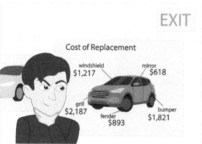

Subtle hints can affect users' decisions

DESCRIPTION:

Instead of forcing users to do something, you can condition them to do something with signs, sounds, and colors.

This can be seen at medical offices where they have posters about every disease that you can think of. Feeling Sleepy? Feeling Tired? You might have StupidNonsense Syndrome. You will also see this at car rental places where they will show you prices of part of car for replacement if you do not buy insurance.

Interesting Fact: Airports are designed in a way to motivate you to "walk" "sit" or even relax by the usage of signs, carpets, and lighting.

Image Above, A customer is refusing a warranty but when he sees a post of a car with the cost of each part that he might have to pay if he doesn't buy a warranty.

7 PROGRESSIVE DISCLOSURE

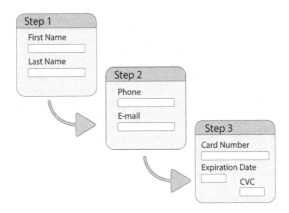

Step 1
First Name
Last Name

Step 2
Phone
E-mail

Step 3
Card Number
Expiration Date
CVC

Users are less overwhelmed if they're exposed to complex features later

DESCRIPTION:

Progressive disclosure is a concept of managing information that dictates that everything in a user interface should progress naturally, from simple to complex. It's a simple yet powerful technique of disclosing information: initially, you show only the most important information or actions and reveal all further options and actions only upon request.

Other Use Cases:

- Checkout Carts: Ask for Name, Email then later Payment
- Software: CRM, EHR
- "Hamburger Menu" On Websites (add hamburger menu icon here)

Image Above, "3 Step Checkout" where they collect basic information first then later ask for more specific valuable questions to close the deal.

FITT'S LAW

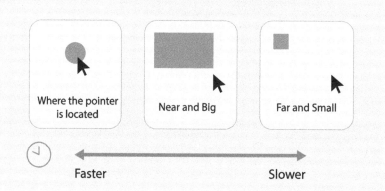

| Where the pointer is located | Near and Big | Far and Small |

Faster ←————————————→ Slower

It's easier to aim the bigger the target is.

DESCRIPTION:

Fitts's Law describes how long it takes a user to hit a target in a graphical user interface (GUI) or other design, as a function of size and distance. Understanding this law helps us design better buttons, forms, lists, and other interactive elements.

It's a useful tool for predicting the time it takes to move from one point to another.

The aim of user interface design should be to reduce the distance from one point to the next and make the target object large enough to enable prompt detection and selection of interactive elements without sacrificing accuracy.

Some Interesting Use-Case:

- Software UI: To reduce the time to click
- Website/ Sales Page: Getting people to buy ASAP

Satish Gaire

9 ATTENTION BIAS

Users' thoughts filter what they pay attention to

DESCRIPTION:

Most airports have a "smoking zone" that non-smokers may not notice at first glance, but smokers instantly find it at first sight.

Attention bias is the tendency to prioritize the processing of certain types of stimuli over others. At any given moment, an individual's senses can perceive countless stimuli in the immediate surroundings.

Interesting Use Case:

- Smoking Zone For Smokers
- Red Stop Sign signals "DANGER"
- Arachnophobia (People Who Fear Of Spiders) Notice the spider first.

Fun Fact: Some research suggests that people with anxiety may have an attention bias, which means that they tend to focus more on threat-related information and less on non-threat-related information. This attention bias may contribute to anxiety by making someone more likely to notice and be worried about potential threats.

EMPATHY GAP

People underestimate how much emotions influence user behaviors

DESCRIPTION:

The empathy gap describes our tendency to underestimate the influence of varying mental states on our own behavior and make decisions that only satisfy our current emotions, feeling, or states of being.

Some Interesting Use-Cases:

- · "Rebound" after a breakup
- · Government commenting on "Unemployment"
- · "Sexual Desire" could cause un-wanted cheating

Image Above, Girl wants to eat healthily but when at the grocery she is buying junk food because her hunger is taking over the logical thing that she should do.

DO SOMETHING AMAZING

Question for you:

If you could do something really nice for a person that you will never meet, would you do it?

Right Now, Go to the site where you purchased this book: Amazon, Walmart, Barnes & Noble etc & leave a honest review about what you think about this book.

This feedback will help someone that you will never ever meet. Because of you, they might pick up this book & make an impact in their life.

Pease take a moment to review this book on AMAZON.

VISUAL ANCHOR

| Elements used to guide users' eyes |

DESCRIPTION:

A visual anchor is a physical object that can be used to provide a reference point for a design. This can be helpful when working on a design that will be viewed from different angles or in different lighting conditions. The anchor can help to ensure that the design is consistent and looks its best from all angles.

Real-Life Use Cases:

- IKEA: Arrows pointing to different departments
- Airports: Walking vs Resting Area
- Highway Billboard telling people where to exit

Image Above, Arrows at department stores give cues on where to go and where they can find certain products.

Satish Gaire

12 VON RESTORFF EFFECT

People remember more items that stand out

DESCRIPTION:

The Von Restorff Effect is also known as the "isolation effect." The isolated piece of information or incident is more likely to be recalled than an event that blends into the background. When something stands out, you point your focus there, and the process of making a strong memory begins.

Real-Life Examples:

- Red is used to highlight important information on a website or document
- A list of items where one item is in a different color or font
- A sign that is a different color from the background

Image Above, A girl is looking at a pricing table and the one that's highlighted and "recommended" with bright color stands out.

VISUAL HIERARCHY

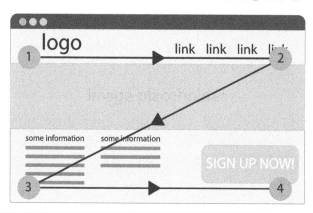

The order in which people perceive what they see

DESCRIPTION:

Website structure is based on where the website owner wants users to look first and where thereafter.

Visual Hierarchy is used to rank design elements and influence in the order you want your users to view them. By using principles like contrast, scale, balance and, more, you can help establish each element in its rightful place and help the most important elements stand out. Simply put, it's the principle of arranging elements to show their order of importance.

Where Visual Hierarchy can be found:

· ECommerce Websites
· Event Flyers: Who/What/When/Where

Visual hierarchy is the most basic form of delivering information and is composed of the following:

· Typefaces and font weights
· Size
· Color
· Style
· Spacing

Satish Gaire

14 SELECTIVE ATTENTION

People filter out things from their environment when in focus

DESCRIPTION:

Selective attention refers to the processes that allow an individual to select and focus on particular input for further processing while simultaneously suppressing irrelevant or distracting information.

Use Case:

- Conversation with someone in a crowded place
- Listening to wife's nonsense from one ear and out the other

Fun Fact: When driving, You are selectively paying attention to the road while ignoring the music playing on the radio.

SURVIVORSHIP BIAS

People neglect things that don't make it past a selection process

DESCRIPTION:

Survivorship bias or survivor bias is the tendency to view the performance of existing stocks or funds in the market as a representative comprehensive sample without regarding those that have gone bust.

Real-Life Examples:

- Businesses only share positive testimonials
- "If I can do it, anyone can" v/s 99% who didn't achieve it
- The cliche saying "Only learn from successful people"

For example, when choosing a mutual fund, an investor might focus on the fund's recent performance and ignore the fact that many similar funds have performed poorly. Or, when considering whether to start a business, an entrepreneur might focus on the success of companies like Google and ignore the fact that most startups fail.

Satish Gaire

16 SENSORY ADAPTATION

Users tune out the stuff they get repeatedly exposed to

DESCRIPTION:

Sensory adaptation is a reduction in sensitivity to a stimulus after constant exposure to it. While sensory adaptation reduces our awareness of a constant stimulus, it helps free up our attention and resources to attend to other stimuli in our environment.

For Example, A person who lives near a train station will notice the sound of the train when it first arrives. But after a while, the sound of the train will become less noticeable. The person has adapted to the sound of the train.

Try This At Home:*

If you put your hand in a bucket of cold water, the initial sensation is quite intense. However, after a few minutes, the sensation decreases as your body becomes used to the cold temperature.

* I am not responsible if the doctor has to cut off your arm or something goes wrong.

JUXTAPOSITION

Two things being seen or placed close together with contrasting effect.

DESCRIPTION:

Juxtaposition in psychology suggest that when people are presented with two contrasting ideas, they are more likely to remember and think about the information.

This is because the contrast between the two ideas helps to create a more distinct memory, which is then more easily retrieved. Additionally, the contrast between the two ideas can also help to highlight the differences between them, making it easier to compare and contrast the information.

SIGNIFIERS

Elements that communicate what it will do

DESCRIPTION:

A pregnant is walking towards everything "pink", indicating that she will be having a baby girl. It's not specifically said but it's implied.

Signifiers are "unspoken" signals that you can pass to make people feel a certain way to communicate a message. It could be colors or already known symbols.

Real-Life Use-Cases:

- · The word "love" can represent the feeling of "love"
- · A heart symbol can represent love or care.
- · A picture of a smiling face can represent happiness.

Image Above, A pregnant is walking towards everything "pink", indicating that she will be having a baby girl. It's not specifically said but it's implied.

CONTRAST

Contrast
in shape

Contrast
in color

Contrast
in size

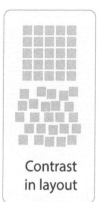

Contrast
in layout

Users' attention is drawn to higher visual weights

DESCRIPTION:

The "contrast" cognitive bias refers to the tendency of the human mind to perceive differences between two objects or concepts to be larger than they actually are. This bias occurs when we compare two things that are different in some way and overemphasize the differences while ignoring the similarities.

This can lead to biased judgments and decisions because we focus too much on the differences and fail to recognize the similarities that may be more important.

For example, a person may think that a new car is much better than their old car because of its shiny new features, even though both cars have similar functionalities.

Satish Gaire

20 EXTERNAL TRIGGER

When the information on what to do next is within the prompt itself

DESCRIPTION:

External trigger psychology is the study of how outside factors can impact our thoughts, emotions, and behavior. This can include things like the media, our environment, and even other people. Our psychological response to these triggers can be positive or negative, and it can affect our mental and physical health.

Did you know this:

Whenever you are watching a commercial for a new car that they really want. The commercial acts as the trigger, and the person then feels the urge to go out and buy the car.

Cognitive Factor

DECOY EFFECT

POPCORN

| Small | Medium | Large |
| $3 | $6.5 | $7 |

decoy

Create a new option that's easy to discard

DESCRIPTION:

The decoy effect is a cognitive bias that occurs when people make a decision based on the presence of irrelevant options. The bias is named for the classic example in which people are more likely to choose Product A over Product B when presented with Product C (the decoy), even though Product C is inferior to both Product A and Product B.

The decoy effect highlights the importance of considering all relevant information when making decisions. It also highlights the power of irrelevant options to influence our choices.

Real-Life Examples:

- Popcorn & Drink Prices at Movies
- Pricing Tiers on Websites
- Insurance and Warranty Plans At Dealerships

Satish Gaire

22 CENTER STAGE EFFECT

People tend to choose the middle option in a set of items

DESCRIPTION:

The Center-Stage Effect is the way in which, when faced with a range or products presented side by side, we tend to be drawn towards the one situated in the middle. ... This central positioning is a social signal that leads us to have a bias toward that particular product and therefore be more likely to choose it.

Classic Cases Of Center-Stage:

- Items place on center shelves at stores
- "Recommended" Plan in the middle of Pricing Tables
- Fashion shows have main model in the middle of others

This shit is used in movies:

The character in the center of the frame appear larger than the other characters. This effect is often used in movies and TV shows to make the main character appear more important than the others.

Cognitive Factor

23

FRAMING

The way information is presented affects how users make decisions

DESCRIPTION:

People decide on options based on whether the options are presented with positive or negative connotations; e.g. as a loss or as a gain. People tend to avoid risk when a positive frame is presented but seek risks when a negative frame is presented.

Real Life Use-Cases:

- Mostly used by copywriters to frame an angle
- Vendors deliberately focus on the positive side
- "0 grams sugar" on chocolates.

Image Above, Both the Yogurt are the same but they use a different angles to convert different things to different people.

Satish Gaire

24 LAW OF PROXIMITY

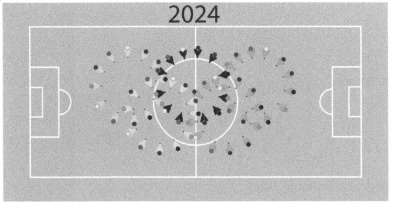

Elements close to each other are usually considered related

DESCRIPTION:

The Law of Proximity, also known as the Gestalt principle of proximity, is a principle in psychology that states that objects that are close to each other tend to be perceived as a group or pattern.

In other words, people tend to perceive elements that are close together as a single group, rather than separate and unrelated items.

EXAMPLES:

In a presentation slide, text that is placed closer to an image or a chart is perceived as being related to it, while text that is farther away is perceived as separate information.

In A Row of circles, the circles that are closest to each other are perceived as a group, while the ones that are farther away are perceived as separate.

---

25   TESLER'S LAW

If you simplify too much, you'll transfer some complexity to the users

DESCRIPTION:

Tesler's Law, also known as The Law of Conservation of Complexity, is a principle in software engineering and design that states that "Every application has an inherent amount of complexity that cannot be reduced or eliminated." This means that no matter what you do, the complexity of a system will always be present, and that complexity cannot be eliminated, only shifted or transferred.

EXAMPLES:

Microsoft Word: Despite numerous updates and features removal, It still remains complex due to its inherent complexity, which cannot be reduced or eliminated.

Medical Devices: Medical devices, such as pacemakers, insulin pumps, and dialysis machines, are designed to be as simple and easy to use as possible. However, the underlying complexity of these devices cannot be completely eliminated, as they must deliver precise and reliable treatment.

SPARK EFFECT

Lose Weight By Running Just 3 Minutes A Day

Users are more likely to take action when the effort is small

DESCRIPTION:

Users tend to take actions that seem small or short. Using this rule will increase the chances users will interact with the product and take an action if it seems easy to produce. This tactic is used to create habit to use a product, or to get people to take action that seems easy enough, but eventually, as they enjoy it, they will do more of it.

Real-Life Case Study:

- **To Form Habit:** Do the Task Just 2 Minutes A Day
- Pre-Filled Information Forms On Opt-In Ads

FEEDBACK LOOP

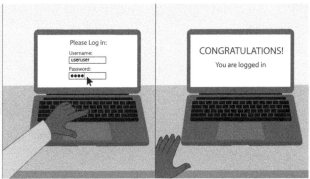

When users take action, feedback communicates what happened

DESCRIPTION:

A feedback loop is a system where outputs are fed back into the system as inputs, increasing or decreasing effects. ****Often feedback and self-correction lead to adjustments varying with differences between actual output and desired output.

Real-Life Example:

- Forget Password, Login Errors
- "Gas Empty" Warning On Vehicle
- Smart Watches Encouraging "More Steps" To Get Lazy People To Walk

Another example of a feedback loop is the regulation of your body temperature. The body's temperature is monitored by the brain, and if the temperature falls outside of the normal range, the brain signals the body to take action to warm up or cool down. The body then takes action to raise or lower its temperature, and the feedback loop continues until the body's temperature is back within the normal range.

---

28 EXPECTATIONS BIAS

> ## People tend to be influenced by their own expectations

DESCRIPTION:

Expectation bias (EB) occurs when an individual's expectations about outcome influence perceptions of one's own or others' behavior. In clinical trials, both raters and subjects may enter trials with expectations. Rater EB occurs when raters expect that subjects will improve over the course of the trial.

Some other examples:

- A person who believes that the stock market is going to crash may interpret any news about the stock market, even if it is neutral, as evidence that a crash is imminent.
- If someone believes that a certain politician is corrupt may interpret any information about that politician, even if it is neutral, as evidence of corruption.
- If someone thinks that a certain product is of high quality may interpret any information about that product, even if it is negative, as evidence that it is of high quality.

Cognitive Factor

29 AESTHETIC-USABILITY EFFECT

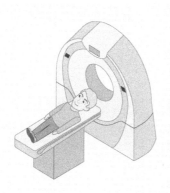

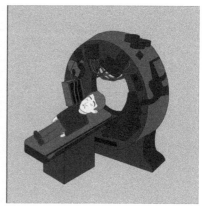

> People perceive designs with great aesthetics as easier to use

DESCRIPTION:

The MRI machine is actually a scary-looking machine but it looks not so scary because of the decoration and plastic on top.

The Aesthetic-Usability Effect (AE) is a principle that a product that is beautiful is generally perceived as being easier to use than a product that is not. This principle is based on research that shows that people tend to judge the usability of a product based on its aesthetics.

The Aesthetic-Usability Effect has been shown to apply to a variety of products, including websites, software applications, and even everyday objects such as tools and kitchen appliances. In general, products that are more aesthetically pleasing are rated as being more usable than those that are not.

This is why beautiful-looking products that seem easy to use are preferred over usable-but-not-beautiful ones or the ones that look "hard" to use.

MEANING

SOCIAL PROOF

Users adapt their behaviors based on what others do

DESCRIPTION:

Social proof is a psychological and social phenomenon wherein people copy the actions of others in an attempt to undertake behavior in a given situation.

Real-Life Use-Cases:

- · Testimonials For Products
- · eCommerce site notifications: "Bob Just Bought XYZ"
- · Hotel Towels Reuse: "Join Others To Converse Climate"

Has this happened to you?

One example of social proof is when people see a long line outside of a restaurant, they are more likely to think that the food must be good and go inside to eat.

Satish Gaire

SCARCITY

> People value things more when they're in limited supply or under time constraints.

DESCRIPTION:

This scarcity tactic is used to show that there is a limited quantity of products or there is a time limit. This creates "FOMO", a Fear of missing out, and gets people to take action, who otherwise would not take fast action. Most of the time, these are "fake scarcity" to get people to buy.

Real Life Use-cases:

- TV Shows like QVC
- "Timer Countdown" On Sales Pages
- Limited Quantity Products

Cognitive Factor 33

CURIOSITY GAP

Users have a desire to seek out missing information

DESCRIPTION:

A curiosity gap is a gap between what a person knows and what they want to know. By keeping information from people, you can create a curiosity gap that encourages them to take action in order to close the gap.

For example, a company might create a teaser campaign that reveals just enough information about a new product to pique people's curiosity, but not enough to satisfy it. This would encourage people to buy the product when it's released in order to learn more about it.

Curious George is a popular children's book character whose curiosity often gets him into trouble. By teaching children about the curiosity gap, you can help them understand why it's important to be careful when they don't know everything about something.

33 MENTAL MODEL

Users have a preconceived opinion of how things work

DESCRIPTION:

A mental model cognitive bias is a type of bias that refers to the mental models or frameworks that individuals use to interpret information and make decisions. These mental models are shaped by personal experiences, culture, and upbringing, among other factors, and can lead to biased thinking.

For example, if an individual has a mental model that associates poverty with laziness, they may be more likely to blame poor people for their economic struggles rather than considering external factors such as systemic inequality.

Mental model biases can be difficult to recognize and overcome, as they are often deeply ingrained in an individual's thinking.

---

34 FAMILIARITY BIAS

People prefer familiar experiences

DESCRIPTION:

Familiarity bias is a type of cognitive bias that refers to the tendency for people to prefer information that is familiar to them. This can lead people to hold on to outdated information and beliefs, even when new evidence is presented that contradicts them.

Real-Life Examples:

- Investment Familiarity Bias: Investing only on stocks you love.
- Going To Same Store For Shopping
- Dating people only from your own culture

Satish Gaire

35 HALO EFFECT

> **People judge things (or people) based on their feelings towards one trait**

DESCRIPTION:

The halo effect is the tendency for positive impressions of a person, company, brand or product in one area to positively influence one's opinion or feelings in other areas. Therefore, it's important not to send the wrong message to distract buyers or audiences.

You might have seen this:

- Celebrity Endorsed Ads: Using Celebrity's reputation for goodwill
- Person On Suit = Rich/Good Person

Did you know this?

If you wear glasses, you are perceived as "intelligent" and seen likable, competent, and trustworthy.

Cognitive Factor

MILLER'S LAW

Hard to remember	Easy to remember

Users can only keep 5±2 items in their working memory

DESCRIPTION:

Miller's Law, also known as the "Magical Number Seven, Plus or Minus Two," is a cognitive psychology principle that suggests that the human brain can only hold a limited amount of information in its working memory at any given time. The theory states that the average person can only retain 7 (plus or minus 2) pieces of information in their working memory at once.

EXAMPLES:

Phone Numbers: Typically phone numbers are seven digits long (excluding the area code) because they fall within the range of numbers that are easy for the human brain to remember.

Passwords: Many websites limit passwords to eight characters or less, which falls within the range of numbers that are easy to remember.

Satish Gaire

37 UNIT BIAS

One unit of something feels like the optimal amount

DESCRIPTION:

The tendency for people to want to complete a unit of a given item or task. People believe there is an optimal unit size and want to get through to the end because they get satisfaction from completing it.

Unit Bias Is Used In Our Day-To-Day Lives:

- · To-Do List
- · Video Courses Modules
- · "Sections" on Forms

Image Above, Girl is happy and satisfied after she has finished her "TO DO" for the day. It gives her sense of accomplishment.

FLOW STATE

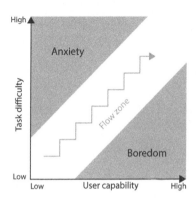

Being fully immersed and focused on a task

DESCRIPTION:

This is the state of being in a flow state. When you are in a flow state you are in a state of optimal performance. You are in the zone and you are performing at your best.

Your brain is working at its highest level and you are able to focus and concentrate on the task at hand. You are in a state of complete absorption and you are completely immersed in the activity.

You are in the moment and you are not thinking about anything else. You are completely focused on the task at hand and you are not distracted by anything else. You can create such state by removing everything that's distracting so that your brain finds the difficult "task" you need to do as interesting enough to actually focus and do it.

Confession: It took me 6 months to write this book because i kept ignoring it because it involved too much thinking, so what i did was, i worked on the book every morning for 2 hrs before looking at my phone. Just coffee and this.

---

39 SKEUOMORPHISM

Skeuomorphism

Flat

> Users adapt more easily to things that look like real-world objects

DESCRIPTION:

Skeuomorphism is a design technique that uses pre-existing design cues to communicate the purpose of an object. In the context of digital design, skeuomorphic design borrows cues from the physical world to help users understand and interact with digital content.

While skeuomorphic design has largely fallen out of favor in recent years, it was once a very popular design style. Many of the most popular iOS apps from the early days of the App Store used skeuomorphic design, including Calendar, Contacts, Notes, and Reminders.

However, you can still use this in marketing and for products by building them to look like things in nature, so people associate it with objects in real life.

RECIPROCITY

People feel the need to reciprocate when they receive something

DESCRIPTION:

Reciprocity is a social norm that involves in-kind exchanges between people—responding to another's action with another equivalent action. It is usually positive (e.g. returning a favor), but it can also be negative (e.g. punishing a negative action).

Reciprocity gets people to do you favor but these have to be fresh Reciprocity or else they are not as likely to return the favor, if you gave them a favor long ago, don't remind them by telling them, instead, use cues.

Real-Life Use-Cases:

- Smiling Is A Form Of Reciprocity
- Free Gifts To Get People To Do Something

Satish Gaire

AUTHORITY BIAS

> Users attribute more importance to the opinion of an authority figure

DESCRIPTION:

Authority bias is the tendency to attribute greater accuracy to the opinion of an authority figure and be more influenced by that opinion. This can lead to people making bad decisions, because they are not thinking for themselves.

Some Use Case:

- Person Endorsing Product With Doctors LabCoat
- Police: People Assume They Are Always Right.
- Following the advice of a financial advisor without question, even if it goes against your better judgment
- Listening to a doctor's opinion without considering other options
- Taking the word of a police officer as gospel, even if you think they may be wrong
- Trusting that a politician will always tell the truth, even if they have lied in the past

Image Above, Author of a book is on stage and everyone believes whatever he has to say because he is an authority figure.

Tasks that are part of a group are more tempting to complete

DESCRIPTION:

Pseudo-set framing is a psychological phenomenon that refers to the tendency for people to see patterns or sets of events where none actually exist. This phenomenon can lead people to mistakenly believe that they have witnessed something paranormal or supernatural, when in reality there is a perfectly rational explanation for what they have seen. Pseudo-set framing is often used by charlatans and con artists to exploit people's gullibility and beliefs.

Its a way of manipulating people by creating a false sense of community. This can be done by using social media to create echo chambers, by holding events that only attract people who already believe in the pseudo-set's beliefs, or by using propaganda to spread the pseudo-set's message.

The goal of pseudo-set framing is to make people feel like they belong to a group, and to make them more likely to believe in and spread the pseudo-set's message. This can be dangerous, as it can lead to people believing in false information, and it can also be used to create division and hatred between groups of people.

43 VARIABLE REWARD

People enjoy rewards, especially unexpected ones

DESCRIPTION:

A variable reward is a reward that isn't always the same. This is usually used in games that have some sort of randomization, such as Loot Boxes or Casinos. Variable rewards are a powerful tool because they create anticipation and excitement in the player. They also keep the player coming back for more, as they never know what they'll get.

Variable rewards can be used in non-game applications as well.

For example, Facebook uses variable rewards to keep users engaged. When you open the app, you never know what you'll see. It could be a news article, a photo from a friend, or a video. This unpredictability is what keeps people coming back.

The most important thing to remember with variable rewards is that they should be valuable to the player. If the rewards are not valuable, then the player will not be motivated to keep coming back.

44 CHEERLEADER EFFECT

Individual items seem more attractive when presented in a group

DESCRIPTION:

The cheerleader effect is a social phenomenon that occurs when people tend to seem more attractive in a group than they are in isolation. This phenomenon is thought to occur because people are influenced by the perceived attractiveness of others in a group. The cheerleader effect is often used to explain why people are drawn to certain social situations, such as clubs or bars.

The cheerleader effect is often seen in social situations, such as when people are in a group setting. For example, people tend to feel more attractive when they are around others, especially if those others are considered attractive themselves. This is because people tend to compare themselves to those around them and feel better about themselves when they are surrounded by people considered to be attractive.

This phenomenon can also be seen in other settings, such as the workplace. Studies have shown that people tend to feel more productive and motivated when they are surrounded by others who are also considered to be productive and motivated. This is likely due to the fact that people compare themselves to those around them and feel the need to match or exceed the productivity of those around them.

CURSE OF KNOWLEDGE

Not realizing that people don't have the same level of knowledge

DESCRIPTION:

The curse of knowledge is a cognitive bias that occurs when an individual, who is communicating with other individuals, assumes they have the background knowledge to understand. This bias is also called by some authors the curse of expertise.

A good example of the curse of knowledge is when someone is trying to explain something to someone else, and they assume that the other person knows more than they actually do. This can often lead to the person providing too much information, or using jargon that the other person doesn't understand.

---

46 AHA! MOMENT

When new users first realize the value of your product

DESCRIPTION:

"The Aha! moment is the moment in a problem-solving session in which one suddenly understands the solution to a problem. The Aha! moment is often accompanied by an exclamation of satisfaction, such as "Aha!", "Eureka!", or "I've got it!". Sometimes, the Aha! moment is preceded by a period of confusion.

To make your product look more valuable, you should include obvious cues that will lead to the "AHA" moment own their own. If you have to tell them about it, its's not going to seem as important.

47 SELF-INITIATED TRIGGERS

Users are more likely to interact with prompts they setup for themselves

DESCRIPTION:

Triggers that are initiated by the individual themselves are deemed to be more helpful in forming habits because they have put in their time/energy to set it up, which is a form of investment.

You can include this on your mobile applications or software to help people use your product more often.

Image Above, Girl receives a notification from a trigger that she set herself.

SURVEY BIAS

Users tend to skew survey answers towards what's socially acceptable

DESCRIPTION:

Survey Bias occurs when people ruin the survey results by not answering truthfully but rather than choosing what's socially acceptable.

For example, if you are asked how often you exercise, you may be tempted to say that you exercise every day, even if you only exercise a few times a week. Social desirability bias can impact the results of a survey by causing people to over-report positive behaviors and under-report negative behaviors.

This is why you should be careful when reading reports from surveys because they might not be what they portray.

49 COGNITIVE DISSONANCE

> Users adapt their behaviors based on what others do

DESCRIPTION:

Cognitive dissonance is a theory of social psychology that describes the discomfort we feel when we hold two conflicting ideas at the same time. The theory is important in explaining why we have a hard time changing our beliefs, even when we know that they are wrong.

The theory was first proposed by Leon Festinger in 1957. He suggested that people have a need for consistency in their beliefs. When we encounter information that is inconsistent with our beliefs, we experience a state of mental discomfort, or dissonance. To reduce this dissonance, we either change our beliefs to match the new information, or we find a way to rationalize the inconsistency.

For example, imagine that you believe that smoking is harmful to your health. You may have read about the dangers of smoking, or seen statistics that show how many people die each year from smoking-related illnesses. However, you may also know someone who smokes and seems to be in good health. This inconsistency between your beliefs and your observations creates cognitive dissonance.

To reduce this dissonance, you may decide to stop believing that smoking is harmful. Or, you may rationalize the inconsistency by telling yourself that the person you know who smokes must be an exception to the rule.

---

50 GOAL GRADIENT EFFECT

Motivation increases as users get closer to their goal

DESCRIPTION:

The goal gradient effect is a psychological phenomenon in which people are more motivated to pursue a goal when it is closer, and the closer they get to the goal, the more motivated they become. The effect is named after the shape of a graph of motivation versus distance to goal, which is called a goal gradient.

This psychological effect has been found in a wide variety of situations, including studies of animals, humans, and even computer simulations. In one famous study, rats were placed in a maze with a food reward at the end. The rats were found to run faster as they got closer to the food, even when the food was not visible.

It is used to explain a wide variety of human behavior, including shopping, gambling, and even exercise. The effect has also been used to design more effective marketing campaigns and to improve customer satisfaction.

Satish Gaire

FEEDFORWARD

MEANING

When users know what to expect before they take action

DESCRIPTION:

Feedforward psychology is an area of psychological research that focuses on how people process and use information about the future. It is based on the idea that people are constantly making predictions about the future, and that these predictions guide their behavior.

One of the key ideas in feedforward psychology is that people use their knowledge of the future to make decisions in the present. For example, if you know that you have a test tomorrow, you might study tonight so that you can do well on the test. If you know that you are going to be hungry later, you might eat now so that you don't have to go without food later.

Use Case:

- · Push or Pull On Doors
- · Elevators

Image Above, The woman is expecting the automatic doors to open as she was near it.

---

52 OCCAM'S RAZOR

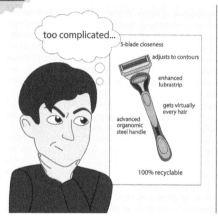

Simple solutions are often better than the more complex ones

DESCRIPTION:

The idea is that simpler explanations of observations should be preferred to more complex ones. This means you should aim to make your products as simple as possible without adding too many bells and whistles.

For Example, A scientist is trying to determine why a particular apple tree produces apples with red skins. After careful observation and experimentation, the scientist narrows down the possible causes to two: either the apples are red because of the type of soil in which the tree is planted or because of the type of fertilizer that is used on the tree.

In this case, Occam's razor would suggest that the more likely explanation is that the type of soil is responsible for the red skins, since this is a simpler explanation than the alternative.

People prefer simple explanations, so so that in your speech, products and sales.

Satish Gaire

53 NOBLE EDGE EFFECT

> ## Users tend to prefer socially responsible companies

DESCRIPTION:

When companies demonstrate social responsibility that is perceived as genuine by consumers, they are rewarded with increased respect, which in turn leads to greater profits.

Real Life Use-Cases:

- · Carbon Offsets Logos On Compay Sites
- · Donation/Charity Photos
- · Doing "Drive for X"

If you run a business, Consider adding "Charity" branch for your company that donates a meniscus amount but you will have the "goodwill" and the bragging rights. Or if you are a consumer, be careful when companies toot their horn.

Image Above, Oil companies bragging about planting trees and good they are doing to make people people over look the fact that they pollute the rivers as well.

HINDSIGHT BIAS

> People overestimate their ability to predict outcomes after the fact

DESCRIPTION:

Hindsight bias, the tendency, upon learning an outcome of an event—such as an experiment, a sporting event, a military decision, or a political election—to overestimate one's ability to have foreseen the outcome. It is colloquially known as the "*I knew it all along phenomenon*."

For example, people often believe that they could have predicted the outcome of a sports game after it has already been played. They may think that they could have predicted that a particular team would win, even though they had no way of knowing this before the game took place.

The bias is often observed in people's recall of events. For example, people may remember that they correctly predicted the outcome of an event, even if they did not actually do so. The hindsight bias can also be observed in people's judgments of events that have not yet happened. For example, people may think that they can predict the outcome of a future event,

---

Satish Gaire

LAW OF SIMILARITY

Users perceive a relationship between elements that look similar

DESCRIPTION:

The law of similarity is a rule in psychology that says that objects that are similar to each other will tend to be grouped together. If two ideas are similar, people will tend to think of them together.

For example, when people are looking for a specific item in a store, they will often look in the section where items that are similar to the item they are looking for are located. The law of similarity is also used in advertising – advertisers often use images that are similar to the product they are trying to sell in order to make people think of the product.

Cognitive Factor

LAW OF PRÄGNANZ

Users interpret ambiguous images in a simpler and more complete form

DESCRIPTION:

The Prägnanz principle is the cognitive principle that states that people will perceive and interpret ambiguous or complex images as the simplest form possible. This principle is also known as the law of good continuation or the law of least effort.

Some examples of the Prägnanz principle at work include:

- · The human brain tends to interpret ambiguous images as faces, even when they are not faces.
- · People tend to see animals in clouds, even when they are not animals.
- · People see letters and words in random patterns, even when they are not letters and words.

Satish Gaire

57 SPOTLIGHT EFFECT

People tend to believe they are being noticed more than they really are

DESCRIPTION:

The spotlight effect is a cognitive bias that refers to the tendency for an individual to believe that they receive more attention from others than they actually do. This phenomenon is often driven by the individual's feelings of self-consciousness and insecurity. The spotlight effect can lead to a number of negative outcomes, including social anxiety, depression, and low self-esteem.

Some Real Life "Spotlight Effects" Examples:

- A search engine highlights the most relevant search results in yellow to make them more visible to users.
- On social media platforms, users often tag friends in photos to get their attention.
- When a user scrolls over a product on an e-commerce website, the image of the product usually becomes highlighted to encourage them to click on it.

Image Above, The guy driving his fancy car thinks everyone is looking at him and his car.

FRESH START EFFECT

> Users are more likely to take action if there's a feeling of new beginnings

DESCRIPTION:

The "fresh start effect" refers to the human tendency to take action towards achieving a goal after a special occasion or key date has passed. We might promise ourselves in January that this is the year we're going to get fit and healthy.

Real-Life Use Case:

· People Starting Gyms In January
· Used In Marketing Angle To Get People To Join A Program

You can use this tactic to offer your product at a specific time, like January when everyone is optimistic about their future or as a consumer you know that the sense of optimism you might be feeling might be because you think this is a clean slate.

Satish Gaire

TIME

59 LABOR ILLUSION

People value things more when they see the work behind them

DESCRIPTION:

The 'labor illusion' means consumers perceive good products more favorably when they're aware of the effort put in but it also makes bad products look worse. So, it's a double edge sword. Use it correctly, and you can show how what kind of hard work goes into a good product, or show how careless the staff is when creating a product.

A lot of restaurants charge a premium when they can see the chefs cook in front of them, this shows "transparency", and increases the perceived value of products.

Companies can implement this on their business by showing "behind the scenes" in form of videos to show prospects the kind of hard work that goes into the product that they are using.

Satish Gaire

DEFAULT BIAS

Users tend not to change an established behavior

DESCRIPTION:

People prefer to take the same route when going places because they are comfortable with that.

This tendency to stay in the default choice is called default bias (or status quo bias) and encompasses people's tendency to choose inaction over action as well as their preference to stick with previously made decisions.

This is a prime reason why people don't want to change parties when voting: A lot of republicans did not like Trump, but they voted for him because "that's what they have been doing" for decades and that's how they were brought up. That was the most comfortable thing for them to do.

Cognitive Factor

INVESTMENT LOOPS

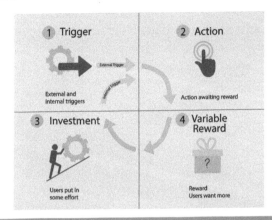

> When users invest in themselves, they're more likely to come back

DESCRIPTION:

Investment Loops is a psychological trick to get people to put an effort on something then offer a random reward that makes them happy. This creates a never-ending cycle of people making efforts for things that might give them a "fake" sense of happiness.

This cognitive bias is used by companies to make their product addicting.

For example, Social media like FaceBook, and Instagram trigger people to take an action, this could be posting the photos they took earlier and then putting them out on their friends' feed, who will comment, and like, which makes the user feel "good", so they start carving the attention even more.

The brain releases "dopamine", a chemical in brain that makes you feel good when you receive a reward. The Cycle continues and their "happiness" is deepened by getting that dose of "notification" or "likes".

LOSS AVERSION

People prefer to avoid losses more than earning equivalent gains

DESCRIPTION:

Loss aversion is a cognitive bias that describes why, for individuals, the pain of losing is psychologically twice as powerful as the pleasure of gaining. The loss felt from money, or any other valuable object can feel worse than gaining that same thing.

This is why "Negative", "Fear Of Missing Out", marketing works because our brains pay more attention to the loss, (however small that is) which makes people make impulsive action wanted by companies and vendors.

Cognitive Factor

COMMITMENT & CONSISTENCY

Users tend to be consistent with their previous actions

DESCRIPTION:

The commitment and consistency bias refers to the idea that people assume less change in their attitudes and beliefs than really occurs. The consistency bias, also known as the commitment bias, is believing one's past and present attitudes are similar.

In other words, we hold on to our initial decision even when we're presented with new information that contradicts it.

This is why when running ads on Google, Facebook, they ask you what your goal is? (Traffic, Conversion etc), because these ad companies know who is more likely to take a certain action regardless of what is presented to them. (So yo burn your ad $ fast)

Satish Gaire

SUNK COST EFFECT

Users are reluctant to pull out of something they're invested in.

DESCRIPTION:

The Sunk Cost Fallacy describes our tendency to follow through on an endeavor if we have already invested time, effort, or money into it, whether or not the current costs outweigh the benefits.

This is why a lot of people stay in bad relationships because they have already spent time in it and they think will lose if they break up. Companies use this technique to make investors invest more money into failing projects since they have already spent money in it and might as well spend more to make sure it doesn't go wrong.

You can use this as a tactic to get your existing customers to buy more products as "upsells" after they have invested the initial amount to get started because the customer will feel as if they might as well spend more money!

DECISION FATIGUE

Making a lot of decisions lowers users' ability to make rational ones

DESCRIPTION:

In decision making and psychology, decision fatigue refers to the deteriorating quality of decisions made by an individual after a long session of decision making. It is now understood as one of the causes of irrational trade-offs in decision-making.

This is why you should not make too many decisions at once because it deteriorates your ability to think things through. Instead, you should opt to 'sleep on it", so you can make a better decision.

As a company, if you wanted to leverage this, you can bombard your clients with multiple decisions and sequence them in a way so that their latter decisions make you the most money.

Satish Gaire

REACTANCE

Users are less likely to adopt a behavior when they feel threatened

DESCRIPTION:

Reactance is unpleasant motivational arousal that emerges when people experience a threat to or loss of their free behaviors. It serves as a motivator to restore one's freedom. The amount of reactance depends on the importance of the threatened freedom and the perceived magnitude of the threat.

When you tell people they cannot do something, the more likely that they will do it. This psychological trick can be used to make people do what you want by making it seem like they cannot.

For example, If you write an email with the subject line: " don't read this email till 11 pm", the chances are people will open it as soon as they get it. You can use reactance in your marketing to get more reaction.

67 OBSERVER-EXPECTANCY EFFECT

> When researchers' biases influence the participants of an experiment

DESCRIPTION:

An observer-expectancy effect is a form of reactivity in which a researcher's cognitive bias causes them to subconsciously influence the participants of an experiment.

This is usually seen in classrooms or at experiments, where the actual person doing the experiment is already expecting something, and participants subconsciously confirm the bias of the researcher. (Sometimes, participants confirm the researcher's bias not wanting to look like a fool) This effect goes hand in hand with "herd affect" as well where people do what others are doing, the only difference on this is that there is an authoritative figure.

As a company, marketers, what you can do is tell everyone that you are an expert in "X" field and go on to make a comment about your bias, then conduct the study, webinar or whatever. This will cause participants to choose what you want.

Satish Gaire

WEBER'S LAW

SUN	Day 1. Run 10 minutes
MON	Day 2. Run 11 minutes
TUE	Day 3. Run 12 minutes
WED	Day 4. Run 13 minutes
THU	Day 5. Run 14 minutes
FRI	Day 6. Run 15 minutes
SAT	Day 7. Run 16 minutes

I can do this!!! It is only 1 min extra a day

Users adapt better to small incremental changes

DESCRIPTION:

The law that the just noticeable difference between two stimuli is a constant ratio of the two stimuli.

This means that if you want to get something done, start with a very minimum effort and just increase it very slowly, this is going to help you build habit and lead you to your desired goal.

This can be used for sales by slowly getting inside your prospect's personal space by interacting in a "non-sales" way to eventually get them to interact with you.

 # LAW OF THE INSTRUMENT

If all you have is a hammer, everything looks like a nail

DESCRIPTION:

The law of the instrument refers to a cognitive bias in which people want to use the same "tool" for every purpose.

According to the *law of the instrument*, when we acquire a new skill, we tend to see opportunities to use it everywhere. This bias is also known as "the law of the hammer", "the golden hammer", or "Maslow's hammer", in reference to psychologist Abraham Maslow's famous quote: "I suppose it is tempting, if the only tool you have is a hammer, to treat everything as if it were a nail"[1].

Keep this bias in mind whenever you are trying to solve a problem because you might not be using the right strategy because you are lenient towards a ONE specific problem-solving method.

Satish Gaire

70 TEMPTATION COUPLING

> Hard tasks are less scary when coupled with something users desire

DESCRIPTION:

Temptation coupling is a phenomenon that says it is more probable for people to do a difficult task when it is coupled with something tempting.

This is a good way to get people to do something that they don't want if you pair it with something that they are happy to do.

Cognitive Factor 73

PARKINSON'S LAW

You Have 30 Days To Do Laundry

Day 1

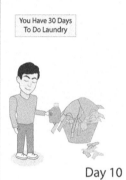

You Have 30 Days To Do Laundry

Day 10

You Have 30 Days To Do Laundry

Day 20

You Have 30 Days To Do Laundry

Day 30

The time required to complete a task will take as much time as allowed

DESCRIPTION:

Parkinson's Law is the old adage that work expands to fill the time allotted for its completion. The term was first coined by Cyril Northcote Parkinson in a humorous essay he wrote for "The Economist" in 1955.

If you tell your prospects that they have 30 days to decide, it will take them 30 days to come up with a decision vs if 3 hours, they will come up with a decision in 3 hrs. You need to urge to take action within a given time limit.

You can also let people have 90 days money-back guarantee instead of 30 days so that the likelihood of them forgetting to request a refund is very low. ☺ (You are welcome)

72 DUNNING-KRUGER EFFECT

People tend to overestimate their skills when they don't know much

DESCRIPTION:

Dunning-Kruger effect, in psychology, a cognitive bias whereby people with limited knowledge or competence in a given intellectual or social domain greatly overestimate their own knowledge or competence in that domain relative to objective criteria or to the performance of their peers or of people in general.

For example, someone who is not good at math may believe that they are better at math than they actually are. This can lead them to make poor decisions, such as choosing a financial investment that is too risky.

People with high ability levels tend to underestimate their abilities. This is because they are more aware of their own limitations and are more likely to second-guess themselves.

AFFECT HEURISTIC

TIME

People's current emotions cloud and influence their judgment

DESCRIPTION:

The affect heuristic describes how we often rely on our emotions, rather than concrete information when making decisions. This allows us to reach a conclusion quickly and easily, but can also distort our thinking and lead us to make suboptimal choices.

The guy in the image above is me. When I am hungry, I want everything on the menu but once I eat a little bit, I instantly regret it. Affect heuristic is important because if you can figure out the emotional state people are in, you can take advantage of them if you want you.

Satish Gaire

> People tend to prioritize immediate benefits over bigger future gains

DESCRIPTION:

Hyperbolic discounting is our inclination to choose immediate rewards over rewards that come later in the future, even when these immediate rewards are smaller.

People want instant gratification rather than delaying happiness for later. If you sell a physical product, mail the product earlier than expected. If you sell the digital item, include an item that they did not include and attach a "value" with it.

CASHLESS EFFECT

People spend more when they can't actually see the money

DESCRIPTION:

The cashless effect describes our tendency to be more willing to pay when there is no physical money involved in a transaction. It means that we are more likely to purchase something on a credit card than if we have to pay for it with cash.

As a company, if you want people to spend more money then you should offer a "Credit" Application right next to big purchase amount. You can also try the "Buy Now Pay Later" model as well.

76 SELF-SERVING BIAS

People take credits for positive events and blame others if negative

DESCRIPTION:

A self-serving bias is the common habit of a person taking credit for positive events or outcomes, but blaming outside factors for negative events. This can be affected by age, culture, clinical diagnosis, and more. It tends to occur widely across populations.

For example, if I make a mistake, I might rationalize it by saying that it wasn't really my fault or that I was under a lot of stress at the time. On the other hand, if someone else makes the same mistake, I'm quick to point out what they did wrong and how they could have done better.

Cognitive Factor

 # PARETO PRINCIPLE

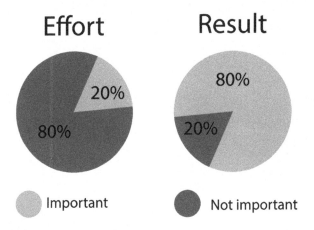

Roughly 80% of the effects come from 20% of the causes

DESCRIPTION:

The Pareto Principle states that for many events, roughly 80% of the effects come from 20% of the causes. In business, this principle is often referred to as the 80/20 rule, and it suggests that 80% of a company's sales come from 20% of its customers.

It can be applied to many other areas of business, such as marketing, where it suggests that 80% of a company's sales come from 20% of its marketing efforts.

The Pareto Principle is a useful tool for identifying areas where we can get the most return on investment. For example, if we want to increase sales, we should focus on the 20% of customers who generate 80% of sales.

Satish Gaire

BACKFIRE EFFECT

When people's convictions are challenged, their beliefs get stronger

DESCRIPTION:

The backfire effect is a cognitive bias that causes people who encounter evidence that challenges their beliefs to reject that evidence and to strengthen their support of their original stance. Essentially, the backfire effect means that showing people evidence that proves that they are wrong is often ineffective, and can actually end up backfiring, by causing them to support their original stance more strongly than they previously did.

Cognitive Factor

FALSE CONSENSUS EFFECT

People overestimate how much other people agree with them

DESCRIPTION:

The false consensus effect, also known as consensus bias, is a pervasive cognitive bias that causes people to "see their own behavioral choices and judgments as relatively common and appropriate to existing circumstances".

For example, people may believe that more of their peers drink alcohol or smoke cigarettes than actually do. This can lead to a false sense of consensus about risky behaviors, which may in turn lead people to engage in those behaviors themselves.

Some people believe in astrology and fortune telling.

DESCRIPTION:

The Barnum effect is the tendency for an individual to personalize a generalization that could apply to anyone. It is a type of cognitive bias that was characterized by psychologist Bertram Forer as being a logical fallacy of personal validation.

This cognitive bias is used to make generalized judgments about people. This is seen usually on "scams" and "Ponzi schemes". If someone is making a judgment on you based on a generalized trait, you should take it with a grain of salt.

IKEA EFFECT

When user partially create something, they value it way more

DESCRIPTION:

The IKEA effect, named after everyone's favorite Swedish furniture giant, describes how people tend to value an object more if they make (or assemble) it themselves. More broadly, the IKEA effect speaks to how we tend to like things more if we've expended effort to create them.

This is the effect companies like "Build A Bear" where people can pick out materials to build their teddy bear or Restaurants like "Ghengis Grill" where you can pick the ingredient to be used for your food value it more.

PLANNING FALLACY

People tend to underestimate how much time a task will take

DESCRIPTION:

The planning fallacy is a phenomenon in which predictions about how much time will be needed to complete a future task display an optimism bias and underestimate the time needed.

An Example of the planning fallacy is when someone doesn't allow enough time to complete a project and then is surprised when they don't finish on time.

One way to avoid Planning Fallacy is to use historical data to estimate the time required to complete a task. This can help to provide a more accurate estimate of the time required to complete a task, as opposed to relying on optimistic estimates which often lead to underestimating the time required.

PROVIDE EXIT POINTS

Invite users to leave your app at the right moment

DESCRIPTION:

1. Products and Applications should have clear exit points to either home page or cart page or for payments or anything that is super important to the benefit of the product.

   Exit points give users a sense of control over their experience, allowing them to close the app or product when they are finished using it, or navigate away from it if they are no longer interested.

For example, Mobile Apps should have Checkout and Payment buttons clearly bright so people can make the payment for their purchases. In many cases, the exit point could lead people back to the "home" so they can restart their journey.

Satish Gaire

84 PEAK-END RULE

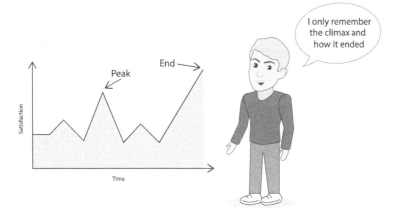

> I only remember the climax and how it ended

> **People judge an experience by its peak and how it ends.**

DESCRIPTION:

The peak–end rule is a cognitive bias that impacts how people remember past events. Intense positive or negative moments (the "peaks") and the final moments of an experience (the "end") are heavily weighted in our mental calculus.

This is why it's important to make your consumers, and clients feel good at the end no matter how sour the journey could have been because people will sum up their experience with you and your company by the "peaks" and how it "ended". A lot of people pay attention to the beginning but they ignore the conclusion, It's super important to make the conclusion of your talk, webinars and writing as good as possible.

Cognitive Factor

SENSORY APPEAL

Users engage more with things appealing to multiple senses

DESCRIPTION:

If you want to make your product much more personalized to the users even before they purchase, you need to make use of appealing to as many senses as possible.

Examples:

1. Food and drink products often use sensory appeal by showcasing their appearance, aroma, and taste through advertising and packaging.

2. Personal care products use the same technique, a perfume commercial may show a woman smelling a flower and then spraying the perfume on her wrist, while a lotion commercial may show someone rubbing the lotion into their

3. An outdoor product for example, a commercial for a camping gear may show the beautiful scenery and the feeling of freedom and adventure, while a commercial for hiking boots may show rugged terrain and the feeling of accomplishment.

Satish Gaire

ZEIGARNIK EFFECT

All projects are divided into actions,

BIG and small.

Even a small incomplete action can affect ALL your open projects.

Completing even the smallest action creates an unconscious commitment to finish a project you're working on.

People remember incomplete tasks better than completed ones

DESCRIPTION:

Named after Lithuanian-Soviet psychologist Bluma Zeigarnik, in psychology, the Zeigarnik effect occurs when an activity that has been interrupted may be more readily recalled. It postulates that people remember unfinished or interrupted tasks better than completed tasks.

The Zeigarnik effect has been demonstrated in a variety of settings and across different age groups. Studies have shown that people are better able to remember incomplete tasks, items on a to-do list, and unfinished stories. The effect has been attributed to a number of cognitive processes, including the need for closure and a focus on the goal of completing the task.

The Zeigarnik effect has been used to explain a variety of real-world phenomena, such as why people are more likely to remember an interrupted conversation than one that they have completed. The effect has also been used to understand why people are more likely to procrastinate on tasks that they find difficult or unpleasant.

Cognitive Factor

ENDOWMENT EFFECT

$2.87

NOT MINE

$7.12

MINE

Users value something more if they feel it's theirs

DESCRIPTION:

The endowment effect refers to an emotional bias that causes individuals to value an owned object higher, often irrationally, than its market value.

This is because people value "their" things more because of the emotional and sentimental value it has over something that's not theirs.

For example, Apple offers to engrave people's name on their Airpods, which make it more valuable to them, because it's theirs. Find ways to personalize the product with consumer's information so that they "feel" as if this is their own and they value it more.

CHUNKING

+14255551212

+1 (425) 555 - 1212

People remember grouped information better

DESCRIPTION:

Chunking is a process by which individual pieces of an information set are bound together into a meaningful whole.

This means that whenever you want to give out information to people, put it into groups of 2-3 words or numbers, this way they are more likely to be able to remember it. This is why companies use those "1-800-CALL-NITE" toll-free numbers to get people to remember it. This should also serve as lesson to you whenever you are giving information to consumers, give it in chunks so that they will remember it.

10%
Text or Audio Only

65%
Text + Picture

People remember pictures better than words

DESCRIPTION:

The picture superiority effect in recognition memory tasks refers to the observation that items studied as pictures are better remembered than items studied as words.

If you want people's attention use images or even emojis, this will create a sense of emotion that's long-lasting. Use this technique on your emails to add emotions, and for other purposes such as branding, or warning signs that you don't want people to miss.

METHOD OF LOCI

Making a Memory Palace

Defining a Path

Encoding the List

Recalling the List

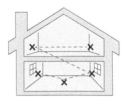

People remember things more when they're associated with a location

DESCRIPTION:

The method of loci is a *mnemonic memory strategy* to help people remember new information in sequential order. The technique involves imagining yourself placing new information around a room and then visualizing going back and picking it up in the order you put it down.

Method of Loci is useful to get people to remember their appointments, or to get kids to remember things or even good if you don't want to forget important things.

SHAPING

Incrementally reinforcing actions to get closer to a target behavior

DESCRIPTION:

Shaping is a technique used in behaviorism to create new habits by reinforcing small, incremental steps towards a desired behavior. The steps are gradually increased in difficulty until the desired behavior is achieved.

For example, if you want to create a habit of running every morning, you might start by walking for a few minutes each morning, and then gradually increase the amount of time you spend running until you are able to run for a full 30 minutes every morning. Reinforcement, such as a reward or positive feedback, can be used to encourage progress towards the desired behavior. Big tech uses this by sending notification or instant gratification by giving rewards or pleasure in shortest span of time. (That's why Short form content like TikTok took off & everyone copied them)

DELIGHTERS

People remember more unexpected and playful pleasures

DESCRIPTION:

To make people like you, your brand, or your "apps", you should send out a message that's unexpected that compliments how they have been doing. This is going to reinforce people to continue to do business with you, this is because people are attracted to positive compliments, especially if they are unexpected. Send these occasionally to have long-lasting effects.

If your company has a software or application, you should send occasional messaging based on their progress, and if you are a sales person, see if you can send these "delighters " to your old prospects who did not purchase from you

---

Cognitive Factor

INTERNAL TRIGGER

When users are prompted to take action based on a memory

DESCRIPTION:

An internal trigger comes from within the person. It can be a memory, a physical sensation, or an emotion. *For example*, if you're exercising and your heart starts pounding, the sensation might remind you of a time you were running from an abusive partner.

Marketers use this to make people imagine an event in your past and then offer you a solution.

For example: "***Remember that last time when you were out in public when you felt anxious because of your severe acne? People ignored who you were but kept staring at your pimples."

With the above sentence, I made the reader evoke past experiences while sitting comfortably at their home, then I can go on to offer the solution.

> *Image Above,* Guy is scared of dogs because of a past event.

Satish Gaire

RECOGNITION OVER RECALL

It's easier to recognize things than recall them from memory

DESCRIPTION:

Recognition refers to our ability to "recognize" an event or piece of information as being familiar, while recall designates the retrieval of related details from memory.

Ever wonder why your wife/GF remembers things about your ex-gf out of the blue when driving by an ice cream place? That's because the ice cream place triggered her to remember an event that occurred that has to do ice cream. That's what "Recognition Over Recall" is.

As a business, what you can do is leave clues on your marketing content, app UI, sounds to trigger people to remember to do something. For example, a Lottery app, plays a "cha-ching" sound everyday at 5 PM reminding you to buy your lottery for the day.

You could even use symbols or objects to remind people about the issues or their to-do things. For example, an image women sweating in sun, might trigger that you need to fix your AC. And you will see their PH# right under the image.

STORYTELLING EFFECT

People remember stories better than facts alone

DESCRIPTION:

When listening to impactful stories, your brain can actually cause you to develop thoughts, opinions, and ideas that align with the person telling the story. If you want people to remember you or your brand, you should tell them a story that sticks with them.

To tell a good story that sticks, you have to make sure it includes the following elements:

Simplicity: Story has to be something simple, no complex characters.

Unexpected: It has to have some kind of surprise factor

Imaginative: People should be able to imagine or compare events to something.

Credible: Somehow the story has to portray that it's legit.

NEGATIVITY BIAS

Users recall negative events more than positive ones

DESCRIPTION:

The negativity bias is a cognitive bias that results in adverse events having a more significant impact on our psychological state than positive events.

This is why marketers remind you of your problems because they affect you more. You can use negative bias to point out issues with people's lives, then quickly show them how your product and service can help them get rid of that "pain".

[*I often tell my customers that, " If they don't buy this, it's ok, they won't be sleep at night wondering what could have happened if they invested on this". Almost always, they call/email me next day asking for "discounts" (they don't want to embarrass themselves). I tell them no, there is no discount, but i tell them that price will go up tomorrow..]

97 AVAILABILITY HEURISTIC

> Users favor recent and available information over past information

DESCRIPTION:

The availability heuristic describes our tendency to use information that comes to mind quickly and easily when making decisions about the future.

For Example, Airplanes are very safe, people might think it's unsafe due to a recent accident that might have taken place, it shows that people use "recent" information as a guiding principle. This means that, as a company, or human being, people will judge you more from the actions that you have recently done rather than something old.

This is also good news for people who want to get rid of their older bad reputation, they can change it by doing a few good things in the interest of public to improve their image.

SPACING EFFECT

People learn more effectively when study sessions are spaced out

DESCRIPTION:

The spacing effect refers to the finding that long-term memory is enhanced when learning events are spaced apart in time, rather than massed in immediate succession.

People are more likely to grasp concepts if there is "time off" between multiple learning sessions. This is why "cramming overnight" usually results in you getting even more confused before tests, so it's better to space them in between.

In marketing, if you are selling high-ticket item ($20-50K+), it's better to space out the marketing emails, and webinars so that the user has the time to process the benefits. If you are teaching a class, you should request users not to read/watch content all at once but rather in small chunk so they can learn it for long term.

Cognitive Factor

SERIAL POSITION EFFECT

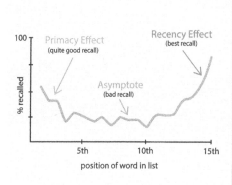

> It's easier for users to recall the first and last items of a list

DESCRIPTION:

The serial position effect is the psychological tendency to remember the first and last items in a list better than those in the middle. The serial position effect is a form of cognitive bias, and it includes both the primacy effect and the recency effect.

People's likelihood of remembering first thing and last thing is much higher compared to remembering things that happened in the middle.

This is why advertising during the world cup or super bowls is more expensive if they are first or at the end because that's what most people remember afterward. So, as a marketer, what you can do is tell people the MOST IMPORTANT thing at the beginning and then fill up the middle with evidence and Talk about the "take home point" at the end.

Satish Gaire

Follow Satish Gaire At

@sgaire

@gairesatish

SatishGaire.com

Get Exclusive Content Online
CognitiveFactor.net